THE ART OF
BULLY MANAGEMENT

PRACTICAL STRATEGIES FOR HANDLING UNWANTED CONFLICT

RAISING FUTURE LEADERS SERIES
MODULE 1

JOSEPH B. ASH

© 2016 by Joseph B. Ash

All rights reserved. No portion of this book may be reproduced in any written, electronic, recording, or photocopying form — except for brief quotations in critical review or articles — without the prior written permission of the author.

Books may be purchased in quantity by contacting the author by email at joe@baeplex.com, or by visiting www.baeplex.com.

Video resources that accompany this book can be found by visiting http://bit.ly/ABMBonus

ISBN 13: 978-0692764565

First Edition

10 9 8 7 6 5 4 3 2 1

Contents

Praise for "The Art of Bully Management .... *v*
Introduction .... *vii*

Awareness 10
Believe 14
Communicate 18
Do Something 22
Educate 26
Forgive 30
Get Involved 34
Help 38
I Am 42
Judge 46
Kindness 50
Listen 54
Manage Yourself 58
No 62
Options 66
Posture 70
Quickly Respond 74
Run 78
Surrounded Yourself in Positivity 82
Team Up 86
Uniqueness as a Strength 90
Voice Yourself 94
Walk Away or Stand Your Ground 98
X-No More 102
Yes I Can 106
Zero Tolerance 110

Appendix A: I Am Words 115
Appendix B: Glossary 117

Praise for
"The Art of Bully Management"

As a school counselor, I often meet with students who feel as though they have been bullied. It is my goal to ensure that my students feel safe, supported, and confident while they are in my care. Through a multitude of programs, we have been teaching students the definition of bullying, how to be an "upstander" and what they can do if they see bullying within our school.

Master Ash goes about giving children, parents, and teachers a way to learn about confidence and how by empowering that primary skill, through the fun use of the ABC's, one can be aware of how to not become a target of bullying. Strengthening your voice, becoming aware of your surroundings, and understanding your safety zones are skills not only for children, but adults as well. Whether on the playground or the parking lot, I believe parents and their children could sit down and learn something from reading this together.

Pamela Kosmowski
School Counselor, West Point Public Schools

"The Art of Bully Management" is a must have, must read and must share family resource on a topic every parent needs to master in today's socially conscious environment.

The book contains an arsenal of tools and techniques for combatting bullying behavior which, as in my case, provided very memorable moments with my children addressing situations they could potentially experience and then practicing powerful responses.

I know eradicating bullying is a long journey, but I also know that my children are far better equipped to manage such situations as a result of this awareness, education and training.

Martyn Canham
Business owner and family man
Houston, Texas

"The Art of Bully Management is an outstanding resource for parents trying to help their children prevent and overcome bullying. Ash condenses a wealth of information into an easy-to-access guide and presents a load of helpful bully management strategies. Highly recommended."

JC Thomas
www.jc-thomas.com
@SuperUltraGo

Introduction

At an early age, I knew I loved people. I had a lot of friends, or at least my parents told me I was always out and about talking with people. Whether they liked me or not, didn't seem to matter. I just loved talking and working with people.

Because I was so small I didn't get invited to play many traditional sports. I was well coordinated, but not picked because of my size and perhaps my overzealous personality. I talked a lot in school, so my parents received many notes and calls about my talking in class. Nonetheless, I always did well in school, so my parents weren't too upset with the talking.

When I was six we moved to the country and I had changed from a public school to a private school. I don't remember it bothering me too much. I remember it was just like before, talking and making friends.

However, shortly after being in the private school, I was teased and bullied pretty severe. Perhaps the most significant instance was on the playground. I was not aware of my new so called friends/classmates surrounding me near the merry-go-round.

Forming a circle around me they proceeded to push from one side of the circle to the other. I remember many of the rude things they were saying to me. Making fun about my clothes, my parents' jobs, and how I looked.

The pushing and teasing went on for what seemed like forever. I remember crying intensely, falling down, and being picked up only to be pushed more. I'm not sure why the teachers ever came, but I remember looking up at the blue sky and seeing it sparkle through my tears.

At one point, I had enough and balled my fist and as I was pushed from one side to another, I took a giant swing at something. All of a sudden the noise stopped and the sky got brighter, or at least that is what I thought was happening. I wiped my tears with my dirty clothes and saw all the kids huddled over the kid that I had hit.

Of course, after that a teacher came and brought us both to the office. I don't really remember what the principal said, nor do I remember what my parents said. The only thing I remember next is starting martial arts with Mr. Bae. The rest is history.

That would not be the only incident I would be bullied, but somehow I had acquired so many skills and strategies from my lessons and class discussions that I was able to deflect or avoid them.

After many years, I began teaching and from there I began helping others through several life challenges. Many of the situations would revolve around bullying. This book is somewhat a brief outline of popular strategies I have seen be the most effective throughout the years.

It is the intent of this book and webinar to empower you with a few simple, yet proven strategies to help minimize or eliminate bullying. Furthermore, it is the aim of this book to be used as a tool for parent-child discussions or even teacher-student discussions. Through open discussions on tough/sensitive topics like bullying, we can navigate the future leaders through the challenges they will face on their way to adulthood.

The Art of Bully Management

Awareness

The Art of Bully Management

Awareness

Before modern technology, there was an intuitive awareness of our surroundings. As we continue to grow faster in our quest for automations and further away from engagements, we lose intuitive awareness. This ability helped keep us alive many years ago. Maybe we aren't faced with angry tribes or hungry tigers out in the wild, but we cannot afford to lose the instinct of awareness.

Survival aside, the awareness of people, things, and opportunities can help us prosper and find peace with various aspects of life. Like that game you play where you highlight the differences in the pictures, you can use that same awareness to know where exits are, acknowledge which objects in the environment may be useful for defense, how many people are in the room, and if needed, what self-defense strategies to use.

Awareness exercise:
1. Do you know how many people are in the room with you at this time?
2. Where are the escape routes located near you?
3. What are some objects near you that could be used to keep distance between you and a bully?

Following Through

Here is where you get to take what you have learned and put it into action. In the blank areas below, write down what you have learned, how you will take action on it, and what you want to see happen as a result.

My Big Takeaway:

My Action Step:

My Desired Outcome:

B
Believe in Yourself

The Art of Bully Management

Believe

Belief and confidence in oneself is the first step in bully prevention. Bullies pester those they perceive to be weaker than themselves. Belief can be seen in how you carry yourself, how you talk, and how much you participate in social activities.

Positive self-talk, or affirmations, are a great way to instill belief in oneself and others. Creating a dialogue with yourself using words and phrases that describe how you would like to feel or be perceived is an empowering habit. Because words are powerful tools, it is important to use words that are empowering. I refer to these phrases as I Am Words.

It is important to note that beliefs can change. Even if you don't believe your statement to be true about yourself at the present time, the rehearsal and conditioning of the dialogue can dramatically enhance the level of belief in oneself.

See I Am Words in Appendix A

Following Through

Here is where you get to take what you have learned and put it into action. In the blank areas below, write down what you have learned, how you will take action on it, and what you want to see happen as a result.

My Big Takeaway:

My Action Step:

My Desired Outcome:

Communicate What's Going On

The Art of Bully Management

Communicate

Speak up! Fear can causes us to shut down and keep things to ourselves. If you cannot speak for yourself, talk to a trusted/concerned friend and communicate what is going on. The key is to find someone you trust, regularly engage with, or that is close to you that can provide you with a safe platform to speak what is on your mind.

There have been many situations when people have felt like there is no one to talk to. In some cases, people have gone to extremes by putting themselves in harm's way for a feeling of isolation, and not talking about their feelings/challenges.

Here are a few ideas of people to consider talking to in times of need:
- Best friend
- Teammate
- Parent/Guardian
- Counselor
- Police Officer
- Neighbor
- Closest Adult or teenager

Following Through

Here is where you get to take what you have learned and put it into action. In the blank areas below, write down what you have learned, how you will take action on it, and what you want to see happen as a result.

My Big Takeaway:

My Action Step:

My Desired Outcome:

The Art of Bully Management

D
Do Something

The Art of Bully Management

Do Something

Doing the right thing can be challenging at times. However, doing something can go a long way in helping others. If your intentions are true, then you can act with confidence that the outcome will be positive and helpful.

As a bystander of a bully situation, taking action by getting help or stepping in can greatly increase the chances of a positive outcome. In self-defense, taking any action is better than no action at all.

Take action often and take action with purpose and persistence.

Following Through

Here is where you get to take what you have learned and put it into action. In the blank areas below, write down what you have learned, how you will take action on it, and what you want to see happen as a result.

My Big Takeaway:

My Action Step:

My Desired Outcome:

The Art of Bully Management

Educate

The Art of Bully Management

Educate

With so many different definitions, it is hard to identify what is actually bullying. As parents it is important to spend the time learning and discussing the definition of bullying, teasing, and hazing. Equally as important is to understand your state laws and regulations governing such issues.

Below are three definitions of what I have found to be consistent and true from my own research regarding bullying, teasing, and hazing.

Bullying:
- Has no age, gender, or race barrier.
- Unwanted, aggressive behavior that involves a real or perceived power imbalance (according to StopBullying.gov).
- The behavior is repeated or has the potential to be repeated.

Can include such acts like:
- Making threats
- Spreading rumors
- Physically or verbally attacking someone

Teasing:
Laughing or criticizing someone in a way that is either friendly and playful or cruel and unkind.

It is important to note here that the deciding factor is intent and context. This is where the area gets blurred and people confuse it with bullying and "kids being kids."

Hazing
The practice of playing unpleasant tricks on someone or forcing them to do unpleasant activities.

Usually associated with teams, clubs, or organizations that test members before acceptance.

Following Through

Here is where you get to take what you have learned and put it into action. In the blank areas below, write down what you have learned, how you will take action on it, and what you want to see happen as a result.

My Big Takeaway:

My Action Step:

My Desired Outcome:

The Art of Bully Management

The Art of Bully Management

Forgive

Forgiveness is the release of burden or guilt from something or someone. Forgiving someone that is trying to harm you can be challenging at times. Even harder could be forgiving yourself. When you can learn to forgive yourself and others you are in essence taking away a negative power.

Self-forgiveness is one of the hardest types of forgiveness. We are our own worst critic and by doing so we limit the true expression of ourselves. Understand that mistakes will be made and wrong decisions will happen. If you can begin to view such experiences as learning experiences, the lightness of life and such circumstances will lift you to a better you.

Forgiveness of others takes courage. If you have a hard time forgiving someone else for the sake of letting them go, then forgive them for the sake of letting yourself go. Keep in mind that most bullies are people who themselves have been hurt and are acting out of somewhat uncontrollable conditions. Having compassion for the pain they are experiencing helps to release the burden from your heart and mind, giving you a sense of freedom and peace.

Following Through

Here is where you get to take what you have learned and put it into action. In the blank areas below, write down what you have learned, how you will take action on it, and what you want to see happen as a result.

My Big Takeaway:

My Action Step:

My Desired Outcome:

The Art of Bully Management

The Art of Bully Management

Get involved

Get involved with programs and projects that foster positive attributes of human nature.

People that engage with others gain the benefit of community, culture, and a sense of belongingness. The feeling of belonging is regularly involved in others have more quality friends within their circle of influence.

Family, friends, and teachers are all good examples of people with whom to interact.

Programs allow for individuals to take part in self-growth and confidence. When done right, programs like martial arts, sports, and recreational activities give the participant the tool necessary to interact and grow.

Projects, on any scale, provide a higher sense of self-worth. Local projects like trash Adopt-A-Road or global projects like water for third world countries all give the participant the sense of contributing to something greater than themselves.

Following Through

Here is where you get to take what you have learned and put it into action. In the blank areas below, write down what you have learned, how you will take action on it, and what you want to see happen as a result.

My Big Takeaway:

My Action Step:

My Desired Outcome:

The Art of Bully Management

Help

Helping those in need is a great way to reduce the impact of bullying. This book highlights several ways to help those in need, but it is important to realize taking action is required. Telling an adult or simply standing beside a friend in need are two great ways to help. They both don't require much interaction from you but go a long way in the outcome.

Some friendly ways to be helpful to those in need:
- Assess the situation with friends
- Stay calm and help others remain calm
- Use positive language and be positive as much as possible
- Provide resources that others may not know
- Anticipate others needs and challenges when possible
- Follow-up and follow through with friends
- Make a buddy system that supports each other

Other helpful resources:
- www.stopbullying.gov
- www.thebullyproject.com
- www.bullying.org
- www.eyesonbullying.org

Following Through

Here is where you get to take what you have learned and put it into action. In the blank areas below, write down what you have learned, how you will take action on it, and what you want to see happen as a result.

My Big Takeaway:

My Action Step:

My Desired Outcome:

The Art of Bully Management

I am

The Art of Bully Management

I am

Bullies are people—and they are hurting inside. This is why they can only prey on people that are weaker than they. Very rarely do bullies confront people that are confident, make eye contact, and that have a voice.

Speaking up in an assertive, yet non-derogatory way, can be the difference between a bully stepping up to you or leaving you alone. Speaking in a tone that exudes confidence and courage and learning to use your voice appropriately sends a message to bullies that you are not someone to push around. Let's be clear: being assertive is not the same as mouthing off. Being assertive means that you speak clearly with a tone that is similar to that of the bully.

Another perspective behind "I am" involves each person believing that they have the right to be who they are inside and out. They can listen to what they want to listen to, think the way they want to think, and dress the way they want to dress. "I am" isn't just about using your voice to speak out, it's about self-expression and standing up for who you are, regardless of what others think.

In order for you to pull this off, you must believe that you are the voice. It takes confidence and courage. Here are two simple action steps to practice using your voice. Two simple practicals:

- Create an "I am" statement (Positive in any area of life)
- Now repeat it and emphasize each word differently. Start by emphasizing "I" and then say the rest of the phrase. Do this three times. Then emphasize "Am" three times. Next emphasize the "____" three times.

Now you should feel different about yourself and your voice.

Following Through

Here is where you get to take what you have learned and put it into action. In the blank areas below, write down what you have learned, how you will take action on it, and what you want to see happen as a result.

My Big Takeaway:

My Action Step:

My Desired Outcome:

The Art of Bully Management

Judge Your Distance

The Art of Bully Management

Judge

We have all heard the phrase, "personal space." Do you actually know yours? Learning your boundaries can provide you with an easy way to identify when you are in danger or at risk. Here are three simple boundaries (we will call zones*) to help you identify your personal space.

Awareness Zone: This is the minimum distance between you and someone/something where you still feel safe or unthreatened.

Caution Zone: This is the area in which you begin to feel uneasy about the distance between you and someone/something.

Danger Zone: This is the point at when you feel threatened or in trouble. Most likely someone can reach you from this distance.

It's important to know that everyone's zones are different and can change with time, age and experience.

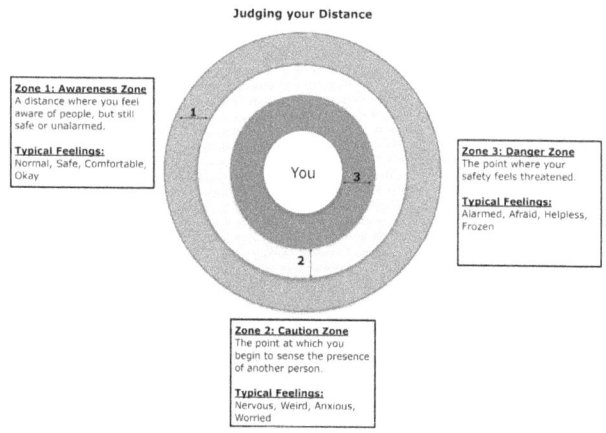

Following Through

Here is where you get to take what you have learned and put it into action. In the blank areas below, write down what you have learned, how you will take action on it, and what you want to see happen as a result.

My Big Takeaway:

My Action Step:

My Desired Outcome:

The Art of Bully Management

Kindness

Shakespeare once wrote, "Kill them with kindness."

In a world bombarded with negativity, a shining light can be kindness. A person or group of people committed to living more out of kindness rather than criticism can bring about a lot of good. Doing your part in the world to share kindness allows for positive energy to flow outward to other people and places.

Being kind not only means towards other people, animals, and things, but towards yourself. When you can be less critical of yourself you become more open to others and other opportunities within the universe. Acting out of kindness allows you to make new friends, help others and make the world a better place for everyone.

Following Through

Here is where you get to take what you have learned and put it into action. In the blank areas below, write down what you have learned, how you will take action on it, and what you want to see happen as a result.

My Big Takeaway:

My Action Step:

My Desired Outcome:

The Art of Bully Management

Listen to Others

The Art of Bully Management

Listen

Be a good listener. You can learn a lot from others by just listening. Allowing others to talk can give you valuable information about what is going on. Being a friend and letting your friend tell you what is going on with them can help you and others figure out how to help.

Kids are short on life experiences and will often turn to a parent, teacher, or mentor they trust to express themselves. At this point, it is important not to judge, but listen to what they are really saying. They are looking for guidance not judgment. Through actively listening you not only teach them that they matter and you demonstrate the power of listening.

Tips to being a great listener
- Focus on the person in front of you, do not be distracted by phone, TV, etc.
- Listen to what they are saying without judgment
- Write down or type what they say - Use the words they use as much as possible
- Ask them to repeat or explain something more if necessary
- Do not interrupt, dismiss or hastily respond
- Ask if it's okay to summarize and once you do ask if what you said is correct
- If you feel like offering advice, ask first. If not, help them find some guidance with a parent, teacher or guardian.

Following Through

Here is where you get to take what you have learned and put it into action. In the blank areas below, write down what you have learned, how you will take action on it, and what you want to see happen as a result.

My Big Takeaway:

My Action Step:

My Desired Outcome:

The Art of Bully Management

Manage

Managing your state can be a powerful attribute in one's life. Often times you become your own worst enemies by speaking with self-doubt, saying you can't do this or that when what you really want is the opposite. Henry Ford once said, "Whether you think you can or you think you can't—you're right."

Managing yourself begins with changing your self-talk. Your voice is the most authentic voice you know. Be mindful of what you say about yourself to others and most importantly to yourself. Start with reciting positive affirmations or sayings to yourself. Listen to and watch positive music and shows that inspire and uplift you. Simply put, if it makes you feel bad, then it's not right for you.

A better way to manage your state is to engage your body and mind. Anthony Robbins often refers to this as, "Making your Move." Although it looks funny or weird, by using your mind and body together, you can change your mood instantly. A simple gesture, like clapping your hands loudly and yelling out a strong "YES!" can immediately snap you back into peak state. Next time you watch your favorite professional athlete, see if they are doing something like this. Maybe they are pumping their fist or pounding their chest while saying something to themselves. Whatever it is, it helps them to get motivated and you can use this same tool to manage your state.

So have fun creating yours and "Make Your Move!"

Following Through

Here is where you get to take what you have learned and put it into action. In the blank areas below, write down what you have learned, how you will take action on it, and what you want to see happen as a result.

My Big Takeaway:

My Action Step:

My Desired Outcome:

N
"No!" Means Leave Me Alone

The Art of Bully Management

No

No is a powerful word. No indicates that something is the opposite of what you desire. When someone says "No," you would think the wishes would be respected. However, the manner in which you say no has a lot to do with whether or not it is received the way you intended. Ideally, saying stop or quit should do the deal, but having a strong no can make a difference in someone challenging you or just leaving you alone.

Clearly identify what you want or don't want will help lead to a better understanding of those around you. However, in the event that you miscommunicate or someone does not adhere to your boundaries, a string clear "No" can put it all to an end.

It is important to remember that you have the power and right to say NO at any time.

Exercise:
Have a parent or friend ask you questions that you would respond with "No." As the questions continue, make the questions pertaining to real life situations.

Following Through

Here is where you get to take what you have learned and put it into action. In the blank areas below, write down what you have learned, how you will take action on it, and what you want to see happen as a result.

My Big Takeaway:

My Action Step:

My Desired Outcome:

Options Are Always Available

The Art of Bully Management

Options

People in danger or stressful situations often feel like there are no other options but to suffer. Time and again people have proven this misconception wrong. There is always a way out. The challenge is being open to other options. Look around and look within to find the answers—options are everywhere. Options are everywhere for you to turn to, hide under, or run to.

Instead of concentrating on what's going on or feeling hopeless, shift your focus to what you want. Shifting your focus will immediately put your mind on a different path. Instead of seeing the problem grow bigger and bigger, you mind will start seeking things that will help resolve your challenge.

You can always shift your focus to other people that have come before you and remind yourself that if they got through it, so can you. A positive affirmation I use for big challenges is: "I am bigger than this challenge."

Following Through

Here is where you get to take what you have learned and put it into action. In the blank areas below, write down what you have learned, how you will take action on it, and what you want to see happen as a result.

My Big Takeaway:

My Action Step:

My Desired Outcome:

Posture

The Art of Bully Management

Posture

How you carry yourself day to day says a lot about your self-confidence. So much of our communication is non-verbal. Even though you may be saying one thing your body language could be saying something else. It seems as though many people have lost the awareness of how they look when dealing with people or in certain situations. Perhaps we were never taught to sit up straight or look another in the eyes when greeting. If so much of what we say is not verbal, we must increase our awareness of body language. Having good body language can make a difference between someone hiring you, being upset with you, or attacking you. Here are a few common tips about the language of posture.

- Keep your chin up and make eye contact when greeting or talking with someone. Not a stare down, but actual eye contact.
- Stand upright like you have a spine, not stiff as a board, but upright.
- Pull your shoulders back.
- Avoid swaying or fidgeting when talking.
- If you shake hands, do so with a firm hand.

Following Through

Here is where you get to take what you have learned and put it into action. In the blank areas below, write down what you have learned, how you will take action on it, and what you want to see happen as a result.

My Big Takeaway:

My Action Step:

My Desired Outcome:

The Art of Bully Management

Quickly Respond with Action

The Art of Bully Management

Quickness

Procrastination is the enemy when it comes to taking action. When something is going on or someone is trying to bully you, act quickly. Duck, dodge, jump, and run quickly to get help. It can make all the difference in your life or someone else's.

The benefit of quickly responding to a bully or self-defense situation is that it has a much greater potential to minimize risk or injury. When responding quickly one also has a better chance of remembering what happened and is more likely to offer better details about the occurrence.

Quickly responding has many positive benefits and here are a few options for possible quick responses:
- Run to get help
- Step in and offer assistance
- Make a phone call
- Tell a friend to get help
- Speak-up

Following Through

Here is where you get to take what you have learned and put it into action. In the blank areas below, write down what you have learned, how you will take action on it, and what you want to see happen as a result.

My Big Takeaway:

My Action Step:

My Desired Outcome:

The Art of Bully Management

The Art of Bully Management

Run

Run! Do not walk when help from a parent, teacher, or friend is needed. If you saw someone lying on the ground hurt from a fall or accident, you would get help immediately. The same level of concern and action must be carried out when you see someone being bullied. Bullying is serious and can cause a lot of bad memories and hurt feelings.

Here is a quick list of some people you can turn to when you witness a bulling situation:
- Parent or guardian
- Teacher or school administration
- Bus driver
- Police officer
- Nearby adult or friend

Following Through

Here is where you get to take what you have learned and put it into action. In the blank areas below, write down what you have learned, how you will take action on it, and what you want to see happen as a result.

My Big Takeaway:

My Action Step:

My Desired Outcome:

S

Surround Yourself with Positivity

The Art of Bully Management

Surroundings

"The best defense is to not be there in the first place." —Author unknown

Look at your surroundings. This is different than awareness. Your surroundings include everything that can be seen, touched, smelled, felt, and heard. A good form of self-defense is to set yourself up to win.

Reading this book is a method of surrounding yourself with positivity. Your overall feelings about this will change over your lifespan, but maintaining control and adjusting accordingly will play a huge part in your ability to thrive in life.

An example could be the music you listen to. Sad and depressing music can bring your spirits down. Instead try something more upbeat, perhaps even electronic instrumental music. We live in a day and age when you can actually pick and choose every song that you listen to. So why take a chance listening to something that may bring you down?

What pictures or phrases do you keep around? Are they inspiring or are they not in-line with what you are striving to feel or be? Imaginations are extremely powerful tools for your psyche. Collect and display some empowering posters, pictures, or drawings that are uplifting and cause a positive shift in your attitude. How are the colors in your room or home? Are they dull and gloomy? Brighten things up. There's science that points to how colors can improve our mood.

Following Through

Here is where you get to take what you have learned and put it into action. In the blank areas below, write down what you have learned, how you will take action on it, and what you want to see happen as a result.

My Big Takeaway:

My Action Step:

My Desired Outcome:

The Art of Bully Management

The Art of Bully Management

Teamwork

Bullies approach people that they think are weak. Teaming up against bullies is a great way to manage. Sometimes it takes more than one person to be involved to deter bullies. Just having a partner, a teammate, or an extra friend around can make bullies think twice about confronting someone.

This is true from a person-to-person perspective as well as community perspective. Schools are a great model where people teaming up to stand up against bullies or not tolerate bullying amongst their peers. If everyone is looking out for one another, then it's harder for bullies to do their work.

Throughout the years, I've adopted the term Power Friends. A Power Friend will stand by your side through thick and thin. He/she will help make you feel good when you don't and take action when necessary.

Power friends have a mutual bond in doing and being good. They may not be your best friend, but are people within your circle that you can rely on. Someone that allows you to feel good about yourself and has no alternative motive.

Exercise:
Exercise: Make a list of your existing Power Friends and those with whom you would like to add to your Power Friend list.

Following Through

Here is where you get to take what you have learned and put it into action. In the blank areas below, write down what you have learned, how you will take action on it, and what you want to see happen as a result.

My Big Takeaway:

My Action Step:

My Desired Outcome:

The Art of Bully Management

The Art of Bully Management

Uniqueness

I believe your uniqueness is your greatest personal strength. Being that we are all different allows us to freely express ourselves in the best possible ways. The world is full of unique things working together. Be happy that you look different, talk differently, and wear different clothes. If everyone were like you it would be a bit boring, right? Your uniqueness makes the world interesting, so embrace it.

When you try to please everyone by being something or someone you're not, it will only lead to frustration and possible lost of identity. Learn to be happy with who you are and how you look. Like elite athletes that stand out amongst the rest, your uniqueness is your strength. Explore it and be happy that you have a special gift to give the world.

Following Through

Here is where you get to take what you have learned and put it into action. In the blank areas below, write down what you have learned, how you will take action on it, and what you want to see happen as a result.

My Big Takeaway:

My Action Step:

My Desired Outcome:

V
Voice Yourself with Assertiveness

The Art of Bully Management

Voice

While sometimes it is better to say nothing at all, if you must say something, voice yourself assertively. Bullies don't like to mess with people that sound and look strong. It is often that simple. Using a strong assertive voice can make the difference between being a victim or not.

Another perspective is choosing the right words or phrases to get a bully to stop or stay away. I am not talking about just having a good vocabulary. I am talking about having a few power words and phrases that are firm, yet non-aggressive for bully confrontations.

Here are a few phrases to practice your voice:
- Stand down — Stay away!
- I am not interested!
- Get away!
- Stop it, NOW!
- Ki Yah!

Following Through

Here is where you get to take what you have learned and put it into action. In the blank areas below, write down what you have learned, how you will take action on it, and what you want to see happen as a result.

My Big Takeaway:

My Action Step:

My Desired Outcome:

The Art of Bully Management

W
Stand Your Ground or Walk Away

The Art of Bully Management

Walk or Stand

Walking away can be an easy way to avoid a bully situation. Walking away is not being weak, rather, taking the high road to not even engage the bully. However, how to walk away and when to walk away can be a challenge. In the end, the best defense is to not be there in the first place. Walking away or taking a stand are both great ways to take away their power and get you to a safer place where they will leave you alone.

When to Walk Away:
- You have good visual contact on the bully.
- The space is safe and open.
- Words are exchanged with little to no physical threat.

How to Walk Away:
- Maintain full view of the bully.
- Move slowly or quickly as situation permits.
- Use your surroundings to get to a safe distance.
- Keep hands free as much as possible.

When to Stand your Ground
- Physical contact has been initiated.
- Supporters are nearby.
- Uncertain of intentions and surroundings.

How to Stand Your Ground:
- Maintain good posture and eye contact.
- Respond assertively but not aggressively.
- Keep calm and be ready for anything.

Following Through

Here is where you get to take what you have learned and put it into action. In the blank areas below, write down what you have learned, how you will take action on it, and what you want to see happen as a result.

My Big Takeaway:

My Action Step:

My Desired Outcome:

"X" Does Not Mark the Spot

The Art of Bully Management

X No More

When it comes to bullying, "X" does not mark the spot. People that are targeted by bullies can sometimes end up feeling like they deserve it. Accepting yourself as a target can lead to making poor decisions and allowing people to walk over you throughout life. Do not accept yourself as a target and do not feel as though you deserve to be bullied. No one deserves to be bullied nor should they reside in the victimhood of being a target.

If you find yourself being a target of bullies get a mentor that you respect and see them on a regular basis. Choosing a mentor can be as simple as asking a teacher you admire. Oftentimes a mentor is not your parent or guardian. They can be a sports coach, sometimes a neighbor, a counselor, or person who you want to be like. A person that has the job or knowledge you aspire to achieve.

If you feel like you are the target of a bully, then it is important to communicate what is going on to your mentor. Examples would be to show someone your Facebook page, cell phone messages, or point them out to a teacher or friend. Declare yourself not a bully and do not tolerate those who make you feel inferior.

Following Through

Here is where you get to take what you have learned and put it into action. In the blank areas below, write down what you have learned, how you will take action on it, and what you want to see happen as a result.

My Big Takeaway:

My Action Step:

My Desired Outcome:

The Art of Bully Management

Yes I Can

The Art of Bully Management

Yes

Someone once wrote the most powerful three words you can say to yourself are "Yes, I Can."

Believing you can do something will help get your through some of life's most challenging times. Truth be told, no matter how much your parents, your teachers, or your friends believe in you, if you do not believe you can do it, it's not going to happen.

A good example of this from my personal life is when I wanted to build my dream facility. About fifteen years before writing this book, I had a crazy dream to build a wellness campus with martial arts as a staple element. I didn't have the resources, the money, the people, or the know how to build anything. All I had was an idea and a strong "Yes I Can" attitude.

For everything that life threw at me, I created a powerful "Yes, I Can" affirmation. Yes, I can bring my dream into fruition. Yes, I can make enough money to support my dreams and my family. Yes, I can make a difference in people's lives. Those "Yes, I Cans," and several more combined with hard work, opened doors to where I am now.

What are some empowering "Yes, I Can" affirmations that can help you through some of your challenges?

Following Through

Here is where you get to take what you have learned and put it into action. In the blank areas below, write down what you have learned, how you will take action on it, and what you want to see happen as a result.

My Big Takeaway:

My Action Step:

My Desired Outcome:

The Art of Bully Management

Zero Tolerance

The Art of Bully Management

Zero

Zero tolerance should be the only tolerance you have when it comes to bullies and friendships. Your circle of friends, including classmates, teammates, and neighbors play a major part in your life, so make it clear to them that you have a zero tolerance rule when it comes to bullying. If you want to feel good about yourself and what you are doing, then you must cultivate positive relationships with people who share your same values about bullying.

Bullies are sneaky and use a combination of verbal, cyber, physical, and psychological tactics to get to their victims. This makes it hard for teachers, parents, and administrators to clearly see all that's going on.

In order to take the wind out of bullying, we must create a culture that does not tolerate it. To create such a culture requires getting more people involved. A community against bullying will make it harder for bullies to victimize others.

Here are three simple action steps to create such a culture:
1. Educate people about the affects of bullying and what resources are available. Example, take a class on bully management at a local schools or a martial arts program. Seek out classes, groups, and organizations where bullying could happen and bring awareness to them. Even though by now everyone knows about our bullying challenge, they need to hear it from different people, at different times, and under different circumstances.

2. Share personal stories about your own bullying experience.

How has it affected you or your family? How have you dealt with the incident since it last happened? Hearing real stories allows others to relate and feel as though they are not alone. This creates more willingness to join the cause.

3. Provide clear actions steps to get where you want to go. Simply stating that a place is a No Bully Zone doesn't empower people with anti- bullying strategies. What is the culture you are trying to create? How do you want everyone to participate in creating that culture?

With more people looking out for one another, we create a more positive and productive environment. This makes it unacceptable for bullies and they will either look elsewhere or change.

Following Through

Here is where you get to take what you have learned and put it into action. In the blank areas below, write down what you have learned, how you will take action on it, and what you want to see happen as a result.

My Big Takeaway:

My Action Step:

My Desired Outcome:

Appendix A

I Am Words

Awesome	Interesting	Quality
Actionable	Ideal	Radical
Amped	Jumping	Righteous
Bold	Jiving	Super
Beautiful	Jokingly	Swift
Blessed	Kind	Speedy
Creative	Kicking	Tough
Certain	Knowledgeable	Tone
Confident	Loving	Transformative
Dynamic	Laughing	Unique
Determined	Liberated	Unforeseen
Destined	Mastery	Unstoppable
Exciting	Marvelous	Virtuous
Everlasting	Mighty	Vibrant
Ecstatic	Noteworthy	Visual
Fantastic	Needed	Worthy
First	Nice	WOW
Free	Outstanding	Warrior
Glamorous	Optimistic	X-Factor
Glowing	Omnipresent	10X
Grateful	Powerful	YES
Happy	Playful	Yearning
Helpful	Precise	Yelling
Humorous	Quick	Zone
Imaginative	Quite	Zestful

Appendix B

Glossary

- **I Am Words:** I am words are prefixes to a statement about oneself, usually positive in nature. Putting the phrase in the present tense tells us how and what we have decided to believe about ourselves.
- **Power Friends:** Positive people that approach work with the same old day routine. This is a term we use a lot at BAEPLEX because it promoted "The same playing field for everyone." Plus, it allows those who are a bit more robust in there energy level.
- **Mentor:** Is defined as someone who helps another learn or grow using their previous experience.
- **Bystander:** Any person who stands by and observes the bullying take place.
- **Bullying:** Bullying is consistent, unwanted, and aggressive behavior towards another. This usually happens where one person has more of an influence, or perceived power, over the other.
- **Teasing:** To elicit a response or provoke someone in an playful way. Can easily be misconstrued as bullying, but normally the intention is not to bully.
- **Victim:** The person often referred to on the receiving end of the bully or attacker.
- **Confidence:** A state of certainty about the truth of something. The feeling of belief that one can rely on someone or something.
- **Self-Esteem:** Confidence in one's own worth or abilities.
- **Resiliency:** The ability to recover or return back to your original state.
- **Leadership:** The ability to gather resources necessary to navigate oneself or a group to a common goal.
- **Citizenship:** Pride in one's status of residence, belief, or culture.

Coming Soon

Here's a sneak peak on upcoming topics for the Raising Future Leaders series:
- Leadership
- Resiliency
- Pride

Joseph B. Ash is available to speak for local groups, teams, and community events. To get in contact with him or his Success Team for comments, bookings, or other related opportunities, e-mail teamwork@baeplex.com.

In his first book, "Martial Arts Unlocked: A Parent's Guide for Choosing a Martial Arts School," Ash, breaks down the many types of martial arts schools. Get an insider's look at how the martial arts business works and a solid punch list of "musts" for a high-quality program direct from the master.

www.ingramcontent.com/pod-product-compliance
Lightning Source LLC
Chambersburg PA
CBHW060815050426
42449CB00008B/1671